Rankin Inlet Ceramics

Curated by Darlene Coward Wight

Essay by Jim Shirley

THE WINNIPEG ART GALLERY

Catalogue of the exhibition *Rankin Inlet Ceramics* organized by
The Winnipeg Art Gallery and presented May 1 – August 3, 2003

National Library of Canada Cataloguing in Publication Data

Main entry under title:

Rankin Inlet Ceramics / curated by Darlene Coward Wight ;
essay by Jim Shirley.

Includes bibliographical references.
Catalogue of an exhibition held at the Winnipeg Art Gallery.

ISBN 0-88915-224-1

1. Inuit art—Nunavut—Rankin Inlet—Exhibitions. 2. Pottery—20th
century—Nunavut—Rankin Inlet—Exhibitions. I. Shirley, James R.,
1944- II. Wight, Darlene. III. Winnipeg Art Gallery.
E99.E7R36 2003   738.089'971207195   C2003-910629-2

Cover image: **Roger Aksadjuak**, *Under the Ice*, 2002

CONTENTS

Director's Preface

PATRICIA E. BOVEY

The Winnipeg Art Gallery is pleased to present this exhibition of recent ceramic work by artists in the Kivalliq community of Rankin Inlet. The creation of work in clay was revived in 1990 under the aegis of the Matchbox Gallery after a fifteen-year hiatus. Veteran ceramists from an earlier period renewed their skills and became teachers to a group of younger artists. This exhibition of recent art by a new generation of Inuit artists is part of on-going programming by The Winnipeg Art Gallery and follows exhibitions held previously, such as Abraham Anghik Ruben (2001), *Germaine Arnaktauyok* (1998), *Between Two Worlds: Sculpture by David Ruben Piqtoukun* (1996), *Manasie: The Art of Manasie Akpaliapik* (1990), and *Out of Tradition: Abraham Anghik/David Ruben Piqtoukun* (1989).

In 1967 The Winnipeg Art Gallery was one of the first public art galleries in Canada to purchase ceramic art from Rankin Inlet. Eight pieces were acquired from a touring centennial exhibition, *Keewatin Eskimo Ceramics '67*, and this number has grown to twenty pieces dating from the period 1964 to 1975. It is appropriate that the gallery has now organized an exhibition revealing the recent results of over ten years of work in clay by the artists of Rankin Inlet.

I would like to express our sincere appreciation to the Matchbox Gallery for the loan of artwork in the exhibition and for the assistance of owner Jim Shirley in the organization of the exhibition. His essay in this publication provides valuable insights into the re-emergence of ceramic art under his encouragement and sponsorship since 1991. We also thank the artists for providing interviews and information for the preparation of the catalogue. I would like to congratulate Darlene Coward Wight, WAG Curator of Inuit Art, for her stewardship of this important exhibition, and for her insight into the work of each of the participating artists.

The Winnipeg Art Gallery also extends sincere appreciation to the Canada Council for the Arts for the financial assistance for the exhibition and publication, to Friesens Corporation for their sponsorship assistance with the publication, to First Air for their support, and to Kivalliq Partners in Development for travel assistance for the artists.

Ceramics in Rankin Inlet:
A Continuing Tradition

DARLENE COWARD WIGHT

Contemporary Inuit art has its beginnings in the 1940s and 1950s in the Canadian Arctic. From the efforts by Oblate missionary, Father Van de Velde, in Kugaaruk to sell ivory miniatures by mail in 1945, to the better-known activities of James Houston and the Canadian Handicraft Guild beginning in 1949, arts and craft items were created for export to southern markets to give economic assistance to Inuit who were facing the transition from a subsistence hunting lifestyle to a cash-based economy.[1] The creation of ceramics in Rankin Inlet has its beginnings in similar circumstances.

The 1940s and 1950s were times of hardship for Inuit in the entire Kivalliq region when a shift in the migration routes of caribou led to starvation among the inland Caribou Inuit. To facilitate the provision of food and supplies, the Canadian government established the communities of Arviat, Whale Cove, and Baker Lake, but Rankin Inlet was formed with a different purpose. It was thought that modern technology in the form of the North Rankin Inlet Nickel Mine would create employment and bring Inuit into a wage-based economy.[2]

The settlement came into existence in 1955 when the mine began construction of its infrastructure, prompted by rising nickel prices during the Korean War. Inuit were brought in from all over the Kivalliq region to participate in this new experiment which introduced them to the skills and lifestyle of hard-rock mining. In 1957 the production of nickel concentrate was begun and for the next five years Rankin Inlet was a boom town. The federal government established the community of Itivia nearby in 1958 to accommodate starving people evacuated from hunting camps. Those residents also moved to Rankin Inlet in the early 1960s.

However, by 1960 it was realized that the ore body would not sustain long term development, and the mine was closed in 1962. There was no plan for people suddenly without jobs, and the government encouraged people to move back to their areas of origin as it wanted to close the community. This was not an option welcomed by many residents and they negotiated with the government to fund the establishment of other employment projects. Several of these, such as a farm that produced chickens, eggs, and pork, and a cannery for seal and whale meat, can be described as unconventional in terms of Arctic economic development. The establishment of an arts and crafts project which focused on the making of ceramics was a happier part of this creative thinking.

In April 1963 Claude Grenier, a fine arts graduate from Chicoutimi, Québec, was hired to organize this new project which had three main areas of concentration: sewing, carving, and the making of works in clay. Although there was a ready supply of carving stone from the tons of stone cleared from the mine,[3] it was a very hard, porous stone and carvers were unable to create the fine details and polished surfaces that characterized stone carving in other communities. The carvers were then encouraged to try the medium of clay, and it is not difficult to imagine the freedom that the malleable clay must have provided those who first tried the medium.

Grenier's experience with ceramics was limited to low-fire techniques only, and to compensate, he encouraged people to "glaze" their pieces with shoe polish. They were then sanded to imitate stone carvings.[4] In December 1965 a selection of these experimental "sculptures in clay" were shown to the Ottawa-based Canadian Eskimo Art Committee, a federal government advisory body for arts and crafts.[5] It was felt that the ceramics were not ready for marketing and there was concern that the figures molded in clay would compete with stone carvings. Grenier was directed to return to the original concept of "the pot" with Inuit motifs and to explore glazes other than shoe polish.[6]

1966 was a year of great momentum. Imported clay was mixed with local clay that had a pebbled texture and could give a variety of clay bodies. The local clay was also mixed with particles of crushed rock to give the ceramic work a unique character.[7] Adorned pots and bizarre human heads with animal parts were hand-built using coil and slab techniques and grew in scale and imagination. Some work was done with low-fire glazes in beige, brown, olive green, blue, and turquoise, but these were not very successful or popular with the artists.

In March 1967 Rankin Inlet ceramics were introduced to the public in the government-sponsored exhibition *Keewatin Eskimo Ceramics*. Featuring 60 works, the exhibition opened at the Toronto Public Library, promoted by a dynamic volunteer organization, the Junior League of Toronto. Two of the artists, Michael Angutituak and Phillip Hakuluk, attended the opening and numerous newspaper and magazine articles appeared.[8] Other artists included in the show were Donat Anawak, Pie Kukshout, Robert Tatty, Joseph Angatajuak, Joseph Patterk, Octave Kappi, Yvo Samgushak, John Kavik, Eli Tikeayak, and Lucien Tutuk Kabluitok. Sales exhibitions were subsequently held at 30 galleries world-wide, including The Winnipeg Art Gallery. Eight pieces were acquired for the Gallery's collection in 1967-68.

In spite of the auspicious start, sales were disappointing from 1967 to 1970, and Grenier resigned in August 1970. The Government of the Northwest Territories (GNWT) took over responsibility for arts and crafts projects at that time, and the Department of Economic Development and Tourism hired Robert Billyard to replace Grenier. Billyard was a graduate from the School of Fine Arts at the University of Manitoba, with a specialization in ceramics, including glazing techniques. He experimented with salt glazes and raku, and the surfaces of the pots became more refined. He was assisted by his former ceramics professor, Charlie Scott, who visited the community in 1973.

A variation of the raku technique which was used in the 1970s is used today by ceramists in Rankin Inlet, as evidenced by several pieces in this exhibition. As with raku, the ceramics are removed from the kiln while they are still hot and plunged into sawdust, which bursts into flame. The black, carbonized sawdust gives a distinctive, although unpredictable, finish to the clay body. Normally the pot is then placed in cold water and the rapid cooling creates a distinctive surface of fine cracks. In Rankin Inlet, however, the pieces cool slowly in a large drum of sawdust placed outdoors. This produces smooth surfaces of carbonized colouration without the surface cracking.

Billyard resigned in June 1973, and Michael Kusugak became the new Arts and Crafts Officer. He had a preference for work thrown on a pottery wheel, but other artists continued to hand-build their pieces. Charlie Scott visited Rankin Inlet again in 1974 and helped Kusugak develop a slip glaze from the local clay which gave a brown surface. A combination of this slip and salt glaze became popular over the next two years. Motifs on the pots became flatter, just slightly raised off the surface.[9] This use of low relief decorative detailing, combined with the use of a slip, has been taught to the second generation of ceramists working today by Yvo Samgushak and Laurent Aksadjuak, who were active until the ceramics workshop officially closed in 1977. The craft shop continued to be a place where people gathered to sell carvings or sewing and to visit until it was finally shut down in 1987.[10]

For 15 years the Rankin Inlet Ceramics Project was a vital part of the community, representing self-reliance and self-respect to many of the people who lived and worked there. It was most appropriate that latent skills were revived by Jim Shirley of the Matchbox Gallery in the late

1980s. Unlike the 1960s, the 1990s was a period of growth in the community. With the signing of the Nunavut Land Claims Agreement in 1993, Rankin Inlet became a political centre and it is now a government headquarters for the Kivalliq region. Unfortunately, interest and support for the arts has not kept pace with these developments. Very few carvings or craft items are purchased by wholesale agencies — the local Co-operative and Northern store — and people must travel "door to door" to sell their works.

Ceramics production is the most vibrant artistic expression in Rankin Inlet today. The Matchbox Gallery provides training opportunities and workshop facilities. Each ceramist is encouraged to explore individual interests in the creation of greenware (unfired clay), and then the technical aspects of firing and finishing become communal activities. This compares to the print shops that have operated in Inuit communities such as Cape Dorset, Baker Lake, Holman, and Pangnirtung. Artists there create original drawings, which are then translated into prints by technicians skilled in the different printing techniques of stonecut, stencil, lithography, and etching.

Currently there are two types of work being done in clay by the ceramists represented in this exhibition: decorated pots and sculpture in clay. Pots are built from thin rolls of clay which are coiled 4 or 5 layers high forming the bottom part of the vessel (see photograph of Roger Aksadjuak, p. 20). This section is burnished smooth and allowed to dry so it will provide solid support for another layer of clay coils. This process is continued until the pot is completed. The exterior of the whole pot is smoothed with sandpaper. Often a terra sigillata slip is applied to all exterior surfaces. Terra sigillata (or "earth seal") is the resultant liquid which separates from the mixture of finely ground clay and water. In the firing it becomes an integral part of the ceramic body, lending itself to a high gloss when hand polished. It allows a single bisque (low temperature) firing of the pot. The application of glazes to clay pots involves a second firing at higher temperatures.

Ceramic pots are usually decorated with low-relief faces and animals by the elder ceramists Evo Samgushak and Laurent Aksadjuak who are continuing the style of work they created in the mid-1970s. Samgushak's *Large Magician's Pot* shows a male and a female face on opposite sides. Elegant fish and whale tails fan from the sides and tops of the heads to give a continuous flow of lines around the whole piece. Lucy Sanertanut's pots also feature human faces, but in higher relief and with more individualized features. The sawdust firing of her pieces contributes to the boldness of her overall designs.

Sculpture and pots merge in many of the pieces by Roger Aksadjuak (*Many Sednas*) and Pierre Aupilardjuk (*Walking with My Father*). Fully three-dimensional figures are applied to the outside of the pots, creating graceful rhythms. These sculptural forms are carefully cut in half, scooped hollow, and put back together before they are applied to the exterior of pots. This gives them a thickness comparable to the pot body itself, so the added pieces fire without cracking or breakage.[11]

Purely sculptural work is also being created by Roger Aksadjuak and Pierre Aupilardjuk. A Repulse Bay-based episode from the legend of Kiviu is shown in Aupilardjuk's *A Man Tries To Save His Brother*. Kiviu is the figure in the kayak who unsuccessfully struggles to pull his brother from the waves. Roger Aksadjuak also enjoys telling stories. His *Couple Rides Pet Polar Bear* is an episode from a film story about a man who raised a polar bear cub as a pet.[12] A playful sense of humour is revealed in his *Four Children Try to Topple Muskox*. *Couple with Seal and Fish* expresses a subtle competition between the man and woman, as each has caught equally impressive game.[13] Roger Aksadjuak moved to Winnipeg in August 2002. He plans to continue his work with clay and looks forward to expanding his creative potential in his new environment.

Jim Shirley sees great promise in the work of the two most recent ceramists to become proficient in clay, John Kurok and Jack Nuviyak. They both have a drawing background, and Nuviyak has begun to create stencil prints. Both make intricately-detailed drawings, and the medium of clay allows them to carry this style into three dimensions.

Kurok explores the expressive potential of the human face: three of his heads are in the exhibition. The scale of *Large Head*, combined with the stark white colour and geometric tattoos, is a statement of power and concentration. *Spirit Wrestler* combines a shamanic head with spirit helper in an unusual composition. Kurok is currently beginning work on masks which focus directly on the human face rather than the full head.

Jack Nuviyak's *Three Magicians* reflects an interest in imaginative and shamanic subjects rendered in minute detail. His works are not strictly narrative and do not tell stories. They are more intuitive and evolve as he hand-molds the clay. His "magicians" have shamanic powers and are autobiographical as they all hold small heads that have been created from clay. One figure holds up a *pana*, or hunting knife, to ward off an unseen thief who tries to steal the clay head in the figure's right hand. Humour is a main ingredient of his work.

Jim Shirley is to be commended for his vision in reviving a ceramics project in Rankin Inlet, and for his perseverance in the face of many difficulties over the last 12 years. He has occasionally managed to obtain training grants, but the day-to-day expenses of his Matchbox Gallery have been an ongoing challenge. As an artist himself, he understands and encourages the most critical element for success: the continuous search for personal artistic expression. This means new materials and techniques to try and new subjects to explore. It is not the easiest approach. Repetition of successful formula is much more commercially expedient, but ultimately leads to boredom among the truly creative. Shirley is well aware of this and so he provides the tools that allow the artists to experiment. The original ceramics project lasted 15 years. There is every evidence that this new endeavour will outlast the earlier one. ∎

NOTES:

1. See Wight, Darlene Coward. "The Handicrafts Experiment, 1949-53," in *The First Passionate Collector/Le premier collectionneur passioné*. Winnipeg: The Winnipeg Art Gallery, 1990, p. 45-92.

2. Onalik, 205-06.

3. Driscoll, 35.

4. Personal communication with Professor Charlie Scott from the University of Manitoba who was invited to visit Rankin Inlet in December 1965 to give advice on glazes.

5. In 1967, the Committee was replaced by the Canadian Eskimo Arts Council which dealt with quality and marketing issues until 1989. See Gustavison for further details.

6. Cook, 60.

7. Nagy, 63.

8. See Bibliography in Neale for many of these references.

9. Smith, 15.

10. Neale, *Inuit Art Quarterly* article, Part 2, 16.

11. Roger Aksadjuak, audio tape interview with Darlene Coward Wight, Winnipeg, March 27, 2003.

12. Ibid.

13. Ibid.

CATALOGUE

LAURENT AKSADJUAK 1935-2002

Laurent Aksadjuak was born in Padlei, a small outpost camp between Arviat and Rankin Inlet. In the late 1950s, he moved to Rankin Inlet to find work at the North Rankin Nickel Mine. After the mine closed, he began to make carvings in ivory and stone for the government arts and crafts project, becoming known in particular for exquisitely detailed ivory miniatures. He soon became involved with the ceramics program begun by Claude Grenier, creating many finely crafted works over the years. One of his early ceramic pieces, a kneeling man with a fish, dating to the 1960s is in the collection of The Winnipeg Art Gallery.

When the Matchbox Gallery began its training program in 1991, Aksadjuak played a critical role in providing technical expertise and stylistic direction to the first group of young ceramists experimenting with their new medium, including his son Roger Aksadjuak. Laurent Aksadjuak used the creation of his ceramics as a means of documenting the nomadic lifestyle in which he had grown up. However, he believed that strong technique was as important as the creative vision of the work.

Aksadjuak was a significant influence on everyone who worked with ceramics at the Matchbox Gallery. Diagnosed with lung cancer in 2001, he continued to work until his death in June 2002. He knew the importance of his ceramics and did some of his best work in the last days of his life.

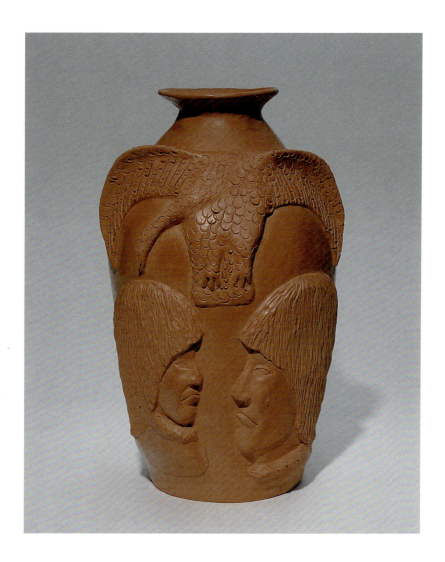

Story Pot 1998

Large Story Pot 2001

ROGER AKSADJUAK b. 1972

Roger Aksadjuak was born in Rankin Inlet, the son of respected carver and ceramist, Laurent Aksadjuak. He has been working as a professional artist since he was 14, and in 1991 he was one of the first of a group of younger artists who began working with clay. Even though he experiments from time to time with carving, clay remains his primary medium. His father was his most important teacher, giving him a firm technical and creative grounding in the medium of clay:

> My father encouraged me to work with clay. I liked it when I started working with clay, with my dad beside me. I learned from him how to make the shape so that it wouldn't break. At one point, he told me that if one piece of clay was almost dry, and the other was too wet, it wouldn't work. It took me some time to understand it. He told me that clay was easier to work with than soapstone. It's easier for me because you can fix your mistake if you make one. With carvings, if you break a piece, you have to glue it. It's never right.[1]

Father and son collaborated on *Spring Celebration*, now in the collection of The Winnipeg Art Gallery. The pot and sculptural figures around the rim were created by Roger and the appliquéd faces around the waist of the vessel are by Laurent. Like his father, he meticulously builds his pots with slender coils, and his imagery is delicately detailed.[2] Some of his pieces, such as *Four Children Trying to Topple Muskox*, reveal a playful sense of humour.

> My father used to work with animals, and this was the work that I liked the best. He told me we had to put stories with them, talking about the way we lived in the past. I keep this in mind and I pass

it along to other people who work with clay.... Inuit who create art should remember that it is an important way that we can be recognized and remembered as Inuit people.[3]

Aksadjuak has work in several private collections across North America. In 1996 he participated in a bronze-casting workshop in Kelowna, B.C. Three ceramic works and a bronze casting have been acquired by the Nunavut Legislative Assembly in Iqaluit for its permanent collection. Aksadjuak was one of two Inuit artists included in a group exhibition of work by twenty Canadian ceramists, *Earth Works: Contemporary Canadian Ceramics*, organized by the Gardiner Museum, Toronto.[4] The exhibition was presented at the Canadian Pavilion at EXPO 2000 in Hanover, Germany June 1 – October 31, 2000, and at the Gardiner Museum February 8 – March 25, 2001. Aksadjuak moved to Winnipeg in August 2002, where he hopes to continue his interest in ceramics.

[1] Interview with Jim Shirley, Rankin Inlet, February 2003.

[2] In an interview with Darlene Coward Wight in Winnipeg, March 2003, Aksadjuak proudly pointed out that the pots by his father are much thinner and lighter than anything he himself has been able to create to date.

[3] Interview with Jim Shirley, Rankin Inlet, February 2003.

[4] Prime Okalik's clay sculpture of a whimsical muskox from the collection of The Winnipeg Art Gallery was also included. Okalik is now living in Whale Cove.

* Work by Roger Aksadjuak and Laurent Aksadjuak

• *Spring Celebration* 2000

Four Children Trying to Topple Muskox 2001

Couple Rides Pet Polar Bear 2001

Couple with Seal and Fish 2002

Skinning a Caribou 2001

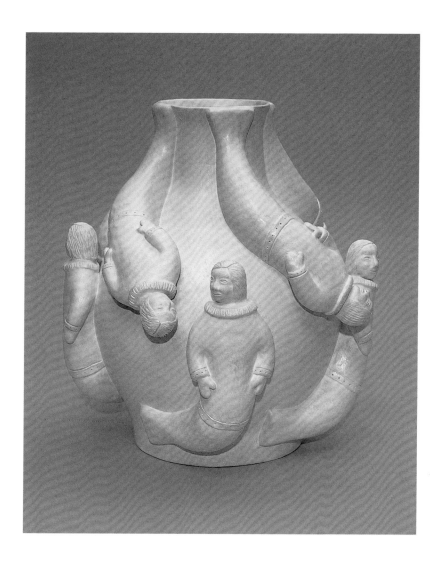

Many Sednas 2002

Birth of a Sedna 2002

PIERRE AUPILARDJUK b. 1965

Pierre Aupilardjuk was born in Repulse Bay, the son of respected carver and elder, Mariano Aupilardjuk. As a child watching his father carve, he revealed an early artistic aptitude. Following a move to Rankin Inlet, father and son were both introduced to ceramics when they took a course at the Matchbox Gallery in the late 1980s. Pierre Aupilardjuk began making ceramics full time during a training program presented by the gallery in 1992. He builds classic vessel forms which are enhanced by sculptural appliqués. His subjects are sometimes inspired by his father's memories of an earlier hunting life on the land and his stories, such as the tales of Kiviu, the legendary figure who traveled widely seeking his bird wife and children. In a recent interview, Aupilardjuk compared carving stone to working with clay:

> You have to be careful about soapstone. When it breaks, you can't fix it. Soapstone can be too soft or too hard in the same piece. With soapstone, you have to work outside as there is so much dust…. [Clay] is easy and soft to work with. When you make it too small, you can add to it….[1]

Aupilardjuk is presently the Assistant Manager of the Ceramics Workshop in Rankin Inlet and gives instruction in ceramics techniques. He has twice been a visiting artist at the Great Northern Arts Festival in Inuvik, and a participant at an Indigenous ceramics festival in Minnesota. He took part in a bronze-casting workshop in Kelowna, B.C. in 1995. In 1999 he was invited to demonstrate his ceramic hand-building techniques at the *Ippaksaq Illuminati — Then & Now* art exhibition in Iqaluit, Nunavut.

[1] Interview with Jim Shirley, Rankin Inlet, February 2003.

Talking About Nunavut II 2002

A Man Tries to Save His Brother (Kiviu Legend) 2002

JOHN KUROK b. 1977

John Kurok has been drawing since he was 8 or 9 years old, and the exquisite detail of his drawing can now be seen in his ceramic work. He began working with clay as a high-school student in 1996-97, and was soon instructing others at the Matchbox Gallery. His particular talent is working with human faces. Masks, busts, and heads are favourite subjects and he works with sensitivity on each piece. He develops a personality for each face, from austere and contained to spirited and youthful.

> *Working in clay was better than working on paper. I like working in three dimensions. When I first started working with clay, I made all kinds of shapes. Then, I started working with faces. I like looking at faces, working with faces that seem to come to life…. When I work with clay, I try to do something different. When you put different things on, it comes out more alive than before. Making animals is my favorite idea in working with clay. Soon, I want to work more with [vessel] shapes with faces and animals on them. I really like Lucy's [Sanertanut] and Pierre's [Aupilardjuk] work. I like Pierre's faces and Lucy's fish.*[1]

[1] Interview with Jim Shirley, Rankin Inlet, February 2003.

Spirit Wrestler 2002

Large Head 2003

JACK NUVIYAK b. 1977

Jack Nuviak was born in Winnipeg in 1977. He has lived all his life in Rankin Inlet except for a year when he was one year old and his family was part of a group of people living at an outpost camp in Wager Bay.

When Nuviyak was a boy he saw his grandfather, Octave Kappi, working in clay. This was after the original workshop had closed. Now Nuviyak enjoys making sculptures from clay, and his hand-molded pieces display a high degree of detail. He says, "I love working in clay and making sculptures."

He first worked in ceramics when he was in high school taking courses at the Matchbox Gallery. After high school, he again studied ceramics in a Matchbox Gallery course sponsored by the Department of Education, Culture, and Employment in 1996-97. He also took the Traditional Arts & Literacy course offered at the Matchbox Gallery in 2000-2001. During this most recent course, he expanded his technical vocabulary in ceramics, and began some new work in stencil print-making and drawing.[1]

[1.] Interview with Jim Shirley, Rankin Inlet, February 2003.

Three Magicians 2003

YVO SAMGUSHAK b. 1942

Yvo Samgushak was born near Baker Lake into the traditional nomadic lifestyle. Although deaf and unable to speak, he earned a reputation as a skilled hunter. A talented carver from an early age, he used these skills when he moved to Rankin Inlet to work in the mine. Although he enjoyed working in ivory and soapstone, by the late 1960s his preferred medium had become clay. He was a dedicated ceramist with the Rankin Inlet Ceramics program in the 1960s and 1970s, and was one of the last people still working when the shop was finally closed in 1977. His brother, Eli Tikeayak, was also respected for his ceramic sculptures and carvings, and another brother, Toona Iqulik, is a well-known carver working in Baker Lake. Laurent Aksadjuak is his brother-in-law.

Samgushak draws heavily from his imagination in creating the distinctive two-headed urns which have become his trademark. His pots often feature enigmatic, shamanistic faces, with fan-like shapes that emerge from the sides of the faces.

Along with Laurent Aksadjuak, Samgushak was responsible for introducing the first group of artists to many of the hand-building techniques used in the Matchbox Gallery studio in the early 1990s. His hand-building techniques continue to have an influence on most of the artists working today.

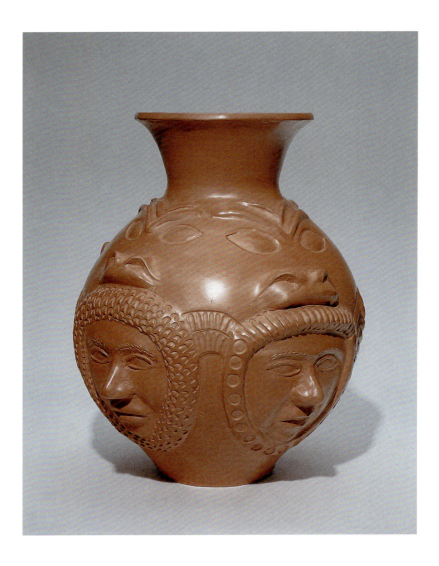

Large Magician's Pot (Four shamans turn into wolves) 1995

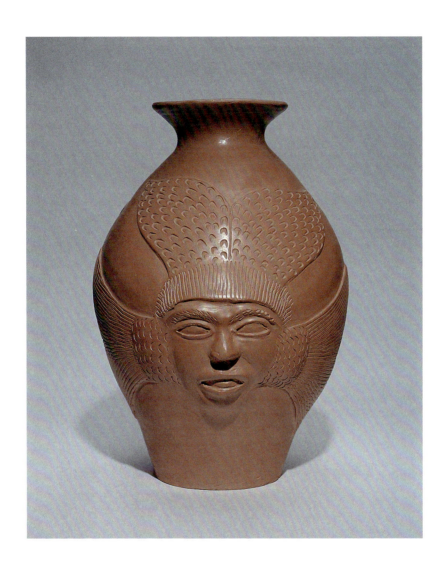

Shaman's Urn 1999

LUCY SANERTANUT b. 1953

Lucy Sanertanut was born in a tent at a camp in the Wager Bay area and lived on the land for her first 13 years. The family then moved to Repulse Bay. Her father taught her to carve when she was 16 years old and she has been carving stone and ivory ever since.

In 1993 Sanertanut, her husband Paul (also a carver), and their four children moved to Rankin Inlet. She immediately began learning ceramic techniques, and found the transition from stone to clay an easy one. She was soon creating complex designs which integrated animals and human elements, particularly faces. She recently discussed her initial interest in ceramics with Jim Shirley:

> When I first started, it was very hard. Pierre [Aupilardjuk] first taught me how to work with clay. I thought about making different kinds of things - pots with polar bears, walrus, seals. After that, Jim [Shirley] told me to try to make faces…. After I learned to make the face, I learned how to make an ear…. I found that I could do it. Clay has made me stronger and more relaxed. When I'm tired and I work with clay, my thinking is stronger. Looking back on it, I think that carvers are better at clay than people who don't do carving.[1]

One of Sanertanut's large pots was awarded first prize for ceramics at the Keewatin Arts & Crafts Festival in 1993. In 1999 one of her smaller vessels was presented to the Minister of Sustainable Development at the Nunavut Tourism AGM. In July 2000, she was an invited artist to the Great Northern Arts Festival in Inuvik where she exhibited her work and demonstrated her clay and carving skills.

1. Interview with Jim Shirley, Rankin Inlet, February 2003.

Faces with Birds 2003

Four Winds 2000

Jim Shirley

Visions & Dreams in Clay

JIM SHIRLEY

The story of the creation of the Matchbox Gallery begins in the Spring of 1979 when I was hired by the Government of the Northwest Territories as an Arts and Crafts Development Officer. My job assignment was to work with artists, crafts people, and arts facilities which had become active in the region over the two decades prior to my arrival. My first excursions through the streets of Rankin were exhilarating experiences, to say the least—the movements and sounds, the smells, the voices and words in a elegant and musical language which rose to meet me on the streets. I had never encountered such wonderful, gifted, and generous people. There was a powerful sense of history and continuity in the voices I heard, and in the ordinary gestures of everyday life.

First Encounters with Old Ideas

A major part of my assignment was to work closely with the Arts and Crafts Centre, located in the old craft shop building; an uninsulated metal structure. Just about every community in the Kivalliq had a similar craft shop. The late 1970s was a wonderful time to be among the people and their art. There was a constant stream of humanity through the shop either to sell or show their creative work, or simply to chat.

I was also intrigued by a ceramics project which had ended just two years earlier. One of the most unusual arts enterprises ever to take place anywhere in the world, it was the starting point for some of our region's finest carvers, seamstresses, and two-dimensional artists. All the artists spoke about it with fondness and with a sense of loss that it had come to an end. These first experiences in the old craft shop formed the genus of a dream that, years later, would become the Matchbox Gallery.

Endings Become Beginnings

As the government began closing the craft shops in the early 1980s, the people who had come to rely on them for their livelihoods were stunned, saddened, and confused. It was a difficult time. But with the collapse of the craft shops, opportunities were created for those who had a vision of the potential of Inuit art which they could now encourage on their own.

The government left behind a rich legacy in its efforts to generate economic opportunities for Inuit. In many communities, the arts and crafts facilities were the centres for more than commerce. There were opportunities for an almost constant dialogue regarding what went before and what was to come, a dialogue in which the unspoken objective was to confirm Inuit cultural strength and resourcefulness. The Matchbox Gallery is very much an attempt to continue that dialogue.

An Idea Becomes A Building

In the mid-1980s my family had been living across the street from Philip Hakuluk, one of the veteran potters from the original ceramics project. I had maintained contact with him and others like Donat Anawak, Laurent Aksadjuak, and Yvo Samgushak, all of them potters who had worked with the original project. I had been asking them, over the years, if they would be interested in continuing to work on ceramics. While there was still some skepticism from the disappointment they experienced in the first project, they all indicated that they would be glad to get back into the work they had been doing years earlier. I had to be certain, if I went ahead with the idea, that I would not disappoint them again.

In 1985-86, when I began to pursue my vision of creating the Matchbox Gallery, I first realized the benefits of being a part of a community. It was our good fortune to be able to purchase an old matchbox building and move it to the space we had leased from the hamlet. The whole operation was done on credit since I didn't really have a dime to my name. Nothing like this could have ever happened in the South. This support inaugurated the good will and the sense of being a part of the community that the gallery has enjoyed ever since. It took about a year to complete the basic renovations needed to make the gallery an operational space. In May, 1987, we had our first opening and display of our prints, drawings, and paintings. Many of the friends who had pitched in to make it happen joined us. It was a day of triumph, a celebration of a community working together with initiative and energy to achieve a common goal that was years in the making.

An Artistic Vision Unfolds

In 1988/89 we received a grant from the Department of Economic Development and Tourism to build a large extension to our existing building which more than doubled our operating space. This enabled us to begin our ceramics and printmaking programs. Our first ceramics workshop began with a group of younger carvers in 1991. Although veterans like Philip Hakuluk and Donat Anawak had passed away, Yvo Samgushak and Laurent Aksadjuak came out of an extended retirement to work once again with ceramics, and to teach our young group of beginning ceramists. I still have memories of Roger Aksadjuak (who has since become a master ceramist and teacher) working at his father's side.

To better prepare for the project, I had enrolled at Concordia

University in 1990 in the ceramics program. As a painter/printmaker, I had very little actual experience in working with ceramics. At Concordia I developed a fondness for the medium and a love for its creative possibilities. I then called on the support of some of the veteran Southern ceramists I had met there, and professionals like Astrid Cruse and Autumn Downey who worked with the Yellowknife Guild of Crafts. Jeannie Sarridge, then working as the Arts and Crafts Development Officer with Economic Development, was critical in getting our program on its feet. We were lucky to have such a skilled professional ceramist in her position. Her guidance and committed support made it all possible.

In 1993, with the help of the Department of Education, we delivered a basic ceramics training program which was tremendously successful, resulting in our first show after only six months of programming. Without the co-operation and support of the government of the time, we would not have been able to establish our ceramics program.

Changing Fortunes

We ran into our first series of challenges shortly after we began to put our work into galleries. Funding and program support was not guaranteed from year to year. Finding ourselves faced with the challenge of providing a regular income for a group of up to eight people without much in the way of outside support, we entered into a working relationship with one of the major distributors of Inuit art. While this was helpful, the pressures of production diminished the focus of our work, and our sales began to decline. Reaching a point where we had to abandon our full-time production, we made the decision to try to survive without government support. Moving from a wage labour to a piecework system, we maintained our group setting for ceramic work. Artists worked only when they wanted to, or when we could afford to pay them.

There were many positive outcomes from this difficult time. We were able to concentrate on perfecting our technical and artistic expertise, took the time to do the best work possible, and called on our artists to focus on new creative challenges. Developing other ways to sustain the gallery besides the sale of work enabled us to collect larger master works which reflected our best efforts. We also encouraged our artists to use their skills in other ways. Many of them began to work as teachers in programs we created at the gallery, and other programs in the community.

The ceramic work produced by the Matchbox Gallery is an extension of how we have worked as a group over the last 13 years, combining the best of communal, traditional learning and applying that learning to a variety of social and artistic outcomes.

Aesthetic Differences

Over the past 40 years, there have been significant changes in the kinds of abilities that people bring to the creative situation. The traditional life involved solving problems with creative thinking, instinct, and strength; qualities that are no longer essential in the modern life people live today. While there is no empirical or scientific basis for it, I feel that there are abilities, based on the challenges Inuit have had to face in their arctic environment, which enable them to bring a distinctive approach to narrative, hand-built ceramics.

A Literacy of Touch

For northern peoples, the ability to manipulate materials, to fashion tools, shelter, and clothing out of limited natural resources, was the cornerstone of their ability to survive. The artwork that comes out of the North, and out of Inuit communities in particular, is a testimony to their abilities at manipulating materials to serve a variety of survival needs. An understanding of the nature of materials, combined with a refined sense of touch, is essential if one is to be effective in working with clay.

A Strong Sense of Spatial Reasoning

I've lost count of the number of times I have been amazed at the ability of Northern people to see objects and animals at long distances. It isn't just a matter of eyesight, it is also careful observation, an essential adaptation for a nomadic people who must be able to see game over long distances if they are to survive. The ability to correctly "read" what is in front of you is also a factor in working with three-dimensional form, whether it is clay or stone. These are the abilities which Inuit bring to their creative efforts that make them some of the world's most naturally gifted artists.

A Communal Approach to Learning

The strength of much of our programming has its foundation in the communally based way that learning takes place. In many ways, it is a replication of a traditional learning system, similar to the one introduced by Claude Grenier when he began the program over 40 years ago. In communicating with each other, people reinforce traditional communications and values. Many problems, particularly among young adults, can be attributed to the lack of a positive environment in which they can learn social skills, and share a positive and supported interaction with others. At the Matchbox Gallery, this kind of sharing of experience is a constant.

There are also many outcomes, aesthetically speaking. Working as a group gives the end results a kind of common approach and communal style. At the same time, the respect for individuality, and for each person finding their own way, is paramount among Inuit ceramists. It is encouraging to see individual differences and styles unfold as each artist achieves their unique command of the medium.

Starting With the Vessel Shape

The basic system we were using when we first began involved sculptural appliqués on vessel shapes. This gave everyone in our program a common starting point for learning basic coil, slab, and pinch-pot techniques in a communal setting. Because people were learning these techniques together, they were able to support each other, and compare their individual approaches to basic hand-building. Working with vessel shapes also helped them to develop a sense for the kinds of forms that are possible with clay. Laurent Aksadjuak and Yvo Samgushak, veterans of the government-run project, gave our group a strong technical starting point. Their advice and personal styles influenced much of our earlier work. Once the artists had confidence and could master basic hand-building techniques, they began to move in more purely sculptural directions, a process which often took years for some individuals to perfect.

Our Struggles with Finishes

Among our challenges, particularly in the beginning, was the use of glazes. While we had some successes, we compromised much of our earlier work by making the wrong choices for glazes. It took us time to realize that our emphasis should be on form rather than surface.

After our experience with glazes, we went through a period in which we simply bisqued our work. It was during this time that we were able to perfect our firing techniques, and to choose clay bodies which best suited our approach. One of the difficulties with our work is the way our ceramists combine varying thicknesses of clay in the same piece. We needed a clay that had good plasticity and enough grog to maintain its shape without cracking. We were successful in finding a low-fire clay body and firing system that worked.

In the mid to late 1990s we began to experiment with terra sigillata, an excellent finish well suited to our work. Because terra sigillata is a single fire system, it enabled us to complete work more quickly, and with less of the risk involved in two firings. It also enabled us to save on our electrical costs (which are substantial in most northern communities). After we became familiar with terra sigillata, we began to experiment with sawdust firing, a system we have found accentuates and enhances the forms in our work. This is a system we are working with quite successfully at the moment.

We have begun to experiment with glazes once again. If we can find glazes that suit our work, we will begin using them on a limited basis in the near future.

The Impacts of Management Styles

It's wonderful to look at the old photos of people working in the original ceramics workshop and marvel at the creative and visionary work that was being done. Those photos were taken by Terry Pearce and John Reeves, photographers then on assignment with the National Film Board, who documented much of the project. Workshop situations express in subtle ways the strategies and aesthetic vision of the managers who run them. Claude Grenier was an extraordinary founder for this artform in the Inuit north. Although I never met him, I get hints of a happiness, a communalism, a sharing of experience that reflected a sensitivity and respect for Inuit culture. The work that was being done shows that Grenier encouraged his artists to experiment and pursue their artistic vision.

Claude Grenier was working with a different kind of artist than the ceramists working today. Since his program was also core-funded by the government, it meant he had access to materials and tools, as well as time in which he could establish the direction of his artists. There were also many more facets to his operation, including the opportunity for artists to work in a variety of media. Much of the work was quite large, a capability which we do not have given our limited resources. Even with all the access and freedoms he must have had in the early days of the operation, I know he ran into difficulties working within the government mandate of the time, which had put a strong emphasis on the project covering it's own costs. When it comes to northern ceramics, creativity and sound business practice are usually at odds with one another.

Financial viability is an issue we have struggled with from the very beginning. It is compounded by the need to pay for the building, the power and heat, the insurance, the materials and equipment, the shipping and marketing, and to pay the artists for their work. I've heard people say that we do this out of some sort of entrepreneurial objective. No sane entrepreneur would embark on this kind of a program!

Our goal, in the management of our ceramics workshop, is to encourage creative vision, craftsmanship, and the proper technical handling of the clay. Examples of the works of aboriginal and contemporary ceramists from around the world are always available. While I have heard comments to the contrary, it would be remarkably narrow to confine Inuit ceramics to a particular predetermined style reminiscent of work that was done nearly forty years ago. I think that the source of much of this pressure to have the work look a certain way comes from the marketplace—a powerful force in Inuit art that has little regard for aesthetic development, and places more emphasis on the relative "value" and demand for the work rather than on the vision of the artist.

Ceramic artists working at the Matchbox Gallery start with their cultural strengths: the narrative capabilities which come from their oral traditions. We want artists to see beyond the physical limits of clay as a medium; to investigate as many levels and layers of their artistic reality as is possible. In order for this to happen, an artist must have a good sense of the strengths and weaknesses of the materials he or she is working with. The stronger their craftsmanship, the more capable they will be of exploring and developing their artistic vision.

As For the Future

I would like to see the project function more as an independent entity, rather than one that constantly needs protection and nurturing as the present project does. Fresh management voices and faces, hopefully from within the present group of artists, would bring it new life. I know that the reality is that this may be a long way off.

We are happy that this project has made its statement as far as the history of Inuit art is concerned, not as some anecdotal activity on the periphery of Inuit creative discovery, but one which occupies its rightful place closer to the centre. Survival is an ongoing struggle for us. Maybe we will "make it," maybe we will not. Hopefully, this show will be a lasting testimony to how we have overcome the odds, and to all the fine work we have done up to now.

I want to thank The Winnipeg Art Gallery for the opportunity they have given me to write this essay. It has provided us with an opportunity to make the development and growth of our project a matter of historical record. We hope our story will inspire other northern communities to do as we have done. ∎

LIST OF WORKS

All works are from the Collection of the Matchbox Gallery, except for *Spring Celebration* by Roger and Laurent Aksadjuak.

Laurent Aksadjuak
1935-2002

Two Couples, 2000
hand-built earthenware,
terra sigillata
36.6 x 28.9 x 28.0

Story Pot, 1998
hand-built earthenware,
terra sigillata
38.6 x 24.0 x 23.5

Large Story Pot, 2001
hand-built earthenware,
terra sigillata
49.0 x 31.4 x 32.3

Roger Aksadjuak
b.1972
Laurent Aksadjuak
1935-2002

Spring Celebration,
1996
hand-built earthenware,
terra sigillata
54.0 x 48.3 x 47.2
Collection of The
Winnipeg Art Gallery
2002-90

Dancing Couples, 2001
hand-built earthenware,
terra sigillata, sawdust
fired
40.0 x 30.5 x 31.2

Roger Aksadjuak
b.1972

*Ptarmigan on Shaman
Bear*, 2002
hand-built earthenware,
terra sigillata
20.5 x 27.3 x 15.3

*Four Children Trying to
Topple Muskox*, 2001
hand-built earthenware,
terra sigillata, sawdust
fired
26.2 x 44.2 x 22.0

Birth of a Sedna, 2002
hand-built earthenware,
terra sigillata
24.0 x 25.7 x 26.6

*Two Men Trying to
Bring Down Muskox*,
1999
hand-built earthenware,
terra sigillata, sawdust
fired
29.5 x 49.0 x 22.0

*Sednas and
Ptarmigans*, 2002
hand-built earthenware
44.5 x 31.2 x 30.6

*Couple Rides Pet Polar
Bear*, 2001
hand-built earthenware,
terra sigillata, sawdust
fired
35.0 x 39.0 x 15.2

Four Dancing Sednas,
2001-2002
hand-built earthenware,
terra sigillata, sawdust
fired
33.5 x 34.1 x 34.5

*Couple with Seal and
Fish*, 2002
hand-built earthenware,
terra sigillata
19.7 x 25.5 x 22.5

Skinning a Caribou,
2001
hand-built earthenware,
terra sigillata, sawdust
fired
12.2 x 29.0 x 23.6

Many Sednas, 2002
hand-built earthenware,
terra sigillata
39.8 x 37.2 x 36.5

Under the Ice, 2002
hand-built earthenware,
terra sigillata, sawdust
fired
41.8 x 30.2 x 32.0

Pierre Aupilardjuk
b.1965

*Walking with my
Father*, 2000
hand-built earthenware,
terra sigillata, sawdust
fired
34.2 x 29.3 x 31.6

Giving Thanks, 2002
hand-built earthenware,
terra sigillata
18.8 x 15.7 x 17.8

*Two Men and Muskox
with Qulliq*, 2002
hand-built earthenware,
terra sigillata, sawdust
fired
20.3 x 28.7 x 18.3

Then and Now, 2002
hand-built earthenware,
glaze
37.7 x 35.2 x 19.0

*A Man Tries to Save
His Brother (Kiviu
Legend)*, 2002
hand-built earthenware,
terra sigillata, sawdust
fired
25.6 x 52.4 x 22.8

*Talking About
Nunavut II*, 2002
hand-built earthenware,
terra sigillata, sawdust
fired
22.2 x 34.2 x 33.3

John Kurok
b.1977

Large Head, 2003
hand-built earthenware,
terra sigillata
34.6 x 28.0 x 28.0

Spirit Wrestler, 2002
hand-built earthenware,
terra sigillata, sawdust
fired
34.0 x 34.8 x 23.3

*Small Head with
Figures*, 2002-03
hand-built earthenware,
terra sigillata, sawdust
fired
22.3 x 16.0 x 21.0

Jack Nuviyak
b. 1977

Three Magicians, 2003
hand-built earthenware,
1) figure with knife:
19.7 x 18.8 x 20.9;
2) terracotta figure:
18.1 x 20.0 x 23.2;
3) figure with four faces:
17.3 x 20.1 x 17.6

Yvo Samgushak
b.1942

*Large Magician's Pot
(Four shamans turn
into wolves)*, 1995
hand-built earthenware,
terra sigillata
42.5 x 37.2 x 36.6

Shaman's Urn, 1999
hand-built earthenware,
terra sigillata
43.5 x 30.0 x 35.0

Lucy Sanertanut
b.1953

Four Winds, 2000
hand-built earthenware,
terra sigillata, sawdust
fired
42.5 x 46.0 x 46.8

Five Dreams, 2000
hand-built earthenware,
terra sigillata, sawdust
fired
28.8 x 36.3 x 30.7

Faces with Birds, 2003
hand-built earthenware,
terra sigillata
24.5 x 28.5 x 18.8

BIBLIOGRAPHY

Becker, Susan. "Keewatin Eskimos work with ceramics." *The Winnipeg Tribune*, July 13, 1968.

Burgess, Helen. "Eskimo Ceramics." *North*, 14, no. 4 (July-August 1967): 42-45.

Cook, Cynthia. "The Question of Authenticity: The Rise and Fall of the Rankin Inlet Project." In *A Question of Identity: Ceramics at the End of the Twentieth Century/Une Question d'identité: La céramique de la fin du vingtième siècle*, ed. Ann Roberts, p. 59-64. Papers from the International Academy of Ceramics 98 General Assembly. Waterloo: The Canadian Clay & Glass Gallery, 1998.

Driscoll, Bernadette. "Rankin Inlet Art: The Winnipeg Art Gallery Collection." In *Rankin Inlet: Kangirlliniq*. Winnipeg: The Winnipeg Art Gallery, 1981.

Grenier, Claude. "Some wonderful, creative years in Rankin Inlet." *About Arts and Crafts*, 5, no. 1 (1982): 28-34.

Gustavison, Susan. *Arctic Expressions: Inuit Art and the Canadian Eskimo Arts Council 1961-1989*. Kleinberg: McMichael Canadian Art Collection, 1994.

Keewatin Eskimo Ceramics '67. Exhibition catalogue with Introduction by W.T. Larmour. The Department of Indian Affairs and Northern Development with The Junior League of Toronto and The Toronto Public Library, 1967.

Kenny, G. I. "Raku In Rankin Inlet." *North*, 18, no. 5 (September-October 1971): 44-47.

Macduff, Alistair. "Through the eyes of a Potter." *The Beaver*, (Spring 1979): 14-15.

Millard, Peter. "Rankin Inlet Ceramics." Review of an exhibition at the Inuit Gallery of Vancouver, April 30 to May 20, 1994. *Inuit Art Quarterly*, 9, no. 3 (Fall 1994): 30-31.

Nagy, Hendrika G. "Pottery in Keewatin." *The Beaver*, (Autumn 1967): 60-66.

Neale, Stacey. *The Rankin Inlet Ceramics Project: A Study in Development and Influence*. Unpublished MA thesis, Concordia University, Montréal, 1997.

Neale, Stacey. "Rankin Inlet Ceramics, Part One: A Study in Development and Influence." *Inuit Art Quarterly*, 14, no. 1 (Spring 1999): 4-22.

Neale, Stacey. "The Rankin Inlet Ceramics Project, Part Two: The Quest for Authenticity." *Inuit Art Quarterly*, 14, no. 2 (Summer 1999): 6-17.

Newman, Nancy. "The Rankin Experiment: Exploration in Clay." In *Rankin Inlet: Kangirlliniq*. Winnipeg: The Winnipeg Art Gallery, 1981.

Onalik, Jimi. "Rankin Inlet." *The Nunavut Handbook*. Iqaluit: Nortext Multimedia Inc., 1998. (Also Website at www.Arctictravel.com)

Shirley, Jim. "Reviving Keewatin Ceramics." *Up Here*, (November 1993): 30-32.

Smith, Louise. *Pottery in Rankin Inlet* (1963 to 1975). Unpublished essay for Eskimo Art Studies course taught by George Swinton, Carleton University, 1975. (WAG files).

Sutherland, Dave. "The Sad Tale of the Rankin Inlet Ceramics Experiment—1963-1975." *Inuit Art Quarterly*, 9, no. 2 (Summer 1994): 52-55.

Williamson, Robert G. "The Keewatin Settlements: A Historical Survey." *The Musk-Ox*, no. 8 (1971): 14-22.

Williamson, Robert G. "Creativity in Kangirlliniq." In *Rankin Inlet: Kangirlliniq*. Winnipeg: The Winnipeg Art Gallery, 1981.

Website

Burlington Art Museum. http://www.virtualmuseum.ca/~fire20/

ACKNOWLEDGEMENTS

Financial assistance for *Rankin Inlet Ceramics* was provided by the Canada Council for the Arts, Friesens Corporation, First Air, and Kivalliq Partners in Development. I would like to thank Helen Delacretaz, WAG Curator of Decorative Arts and Contemporary Fine Craft, for her advice and valuable assistance with the installation of the exhibition. Charlie Scott of the University if Manitoba provided information about the early period of ceramic production. The artists were most gracious in providing information to both Jim Shirley and me and traveled to Winnipeg for the opening of the exhibition. Finally, my thanks to Jim Shirley of the Matchbox Gallery for his insightful essay, for biographical information on the artists, for fund-raising and organizing travel to Winnipeg for the opening, and for the loan of several works in the exhibition.

Darlene Coward Wight

CREDITS

Photography of artworks: Ernest Mayer

Photography of artists: Jim Shirley

Editing: Heather Mousseau

Catalogue design: Frank Reimer

Prepress and printing: Friesens Corporation

Rankin Inlet Ceramics is made possible with a grant from the Canada Council for the Arts, the generous sponsorship of Friesens Corporation, and support from First Air and Kivalliq Partners in Development.

Printed in Canada

THE WINNIPEG ART GALLERY
Involving People In The Visual Arts

300 Memorial Blvd. Winnipeg, Manitoba R3C 1V1
Tel.: (204) 786-6641 Web: www.wag.mb.ca